Resistance Poetry 2

International Festival of Poetry of Resistance, Anthology 2012, Toronto

Resistance Poetry 2

International Festival of Poetry of Resistance, Anthology 2012, Toronto

Editor

Roger Langen

First Edition

Hidden Brook Press
www.HiddenBrookPress.com
writers@HiddenBrookPress.com

Copyright © 2012 Hidden Brook Press
Copyright © 2012 IFPOR

All rights for poems revert to the authors. All rights for book layout and design revert to Hidden Brook Press. No part of this book may be reproduced except by a reviewer who may quote brief passages in a review. The use of any part of this publication reproduced, transmitted in any form or by any means, electronic, mechanical, photocopied, recorded or otherwise stored in a retrieval system without prior written consent of the publisher is an infringement of the copyright law.

Resistance Poetry 2
International Festival of Poetry of Resistance, Anthology 2012, Toronto

Editor – Roger Langen
Front and Back Cover Art – Gabriele Brossard
Cover Design – Richard M. Grove
Layout and Design – Richard M. Grove

Co-Coordinators of IFPOR 4 – Patrick Connors and Jeannine Pitas

Typeset in Papyrus

Printed and bound in USA

Library and Archives Canada Cataloguing in Publication

   Resistance poetry 2 : International Festival of Poetry of
Resistance, Anthology 2012, Toronto / editor, Roger Langen.

ISBN 978-1-897475-90-4

   1. Political poetry. 2. Protest poetry. I. Langen, Roger, 1949-
II. Title: Resistance poetry two.

PN6110.P728R47 2012   808.81'9358   C2012-905472-0

Dedicated to the memory of
Daniel del Solar
and
Roberto González

Table of Contents

James Sugiyama – Tourist in Africville, Migration – *p. 1, 3*
Michelle Mae Sutherland – No Canadian Experience – *p. 4*
Jorge Etcheverry Arcaya – Ready & Reddish, Analogy – *p. 6, 7*
Don Weitz – Nameless-Homeless (a rant in progress) – *p. 8*
Kenji Tokawa – Race – *p. 11*
Osaze Dolabaille – The Power of One, Silent Too Long – *p. 15, 18*
Mahlikah Awe:ri – Dying Breed – *p. 19*
Candace Dube – The Same Night – *p. 22*
Alys Skel – Ode to Mumia Abu-Jamal – *p. 24*
Ariel David – Metro West, Physical intrusion, The one who left his mind at the station, Overdose – *p. 25, 27, 28, 29*
Jeannine Pitas – Czeslaw Milosz, Proof, No más muertes – *p. 30, 32, 33*
Patrick Connors – An Open Letter to the Prime Minister – *p. 34*
Tom Smarda – Horror Story, Floor Tiles – *p. 36, 37*
Soheila Pashang – Suitcase, Dream – *p. 38, 40*
Rashidah Ismaili – Attar and Tamirs – *p. 41*
Tomás Aquilino López – The Unwritten Song – *p. 44*
Katharine Beeman – What you don't see from the North, Rap for the Five, Coming home poem / La Puerta – *p. 45, 46, 47*
Antonio Guerrero Rodriguez – To Love Life – *p. 48*
James Cockcroft – 'Daniel vive, carajo!' – *p. 50*
Ramon Labañino Salazar – Poem to a Brother – *p. 53*
Lisa Makarchuk – Lest We Forget – *p. 54*
Bengt Berg – Power Lines – *p. 56*
Marilyn Lerch – As the Earth Burns – *p. 57*
Philip Cairns – Bombing for Peace – *p. 60*
Elizabeth Hill – Assumptions Are Made – *p. 63*
Veronica Eley – Grey Blanket, Feelings, Gerstein Centre – *p. 64, 66, 67*
Roger Langen – Life's mysteries, A short history of the world in drink, For peat's sake, French-Maliseet-Irish et cetera – *p. 68, 69, 70, 71*

Words should minister to matter.

Robert Burton

Foreword

The theme, Against State Terror, accords well with the origins of our little book – Medellin, Colombia, 1991. In that year and place, 13 Colombian poets, defying the spiritual decay in their country and the violent reputation of their city, recited poems "in resistance" before an audience of 1,500 at the First International Poetry Festival of Medellin. There have been 21 such festivals since. Out of the Medellin experience, a World Poetry Movement has been spawned.

The 4th International Festival of the Poetry of Resistance Toronto, and the IFPOR 2nd Anthology, *Resistance Poetry 2*, is but a single articulation in this rather surprising global upsurge in the re-assertion of human dignity under the banner of poetry.

Or is it so surprising? Poetry is a form of "insurgency," writes a contributor to the IFPOR 1st Anthology, *Poetry of Resistance:*

poetry is the beautiful bullet that kills no one
the sword of the spirit that slays ignorance and despair
an arsenal of words to break the mind open
re-building hearts, as houses to put hope in

What is the matter to which words should minister if not – according to the 17th century librarian Robert Burton – the "streams of blood able to turn mills"? The metaphor of an industry propelled by the gushing expenditure of human lives is apt today. Think Colombia. Or the American adventure just about anywhere, as Lisa Makarchuk reminds Hillary Clinton in her poem, *Lest We Forget*.

Out of the ground of the innocent dead spring the flowers of truth and memory we call poems. Such poems are not only words that matter but a mode of resistance in themselves. To recall or praise one lost, as James Cockcroft does in his *in memoriam* poem to Daniel del Solar; to evoke the memory of a displaced community, as James Sugiyama in

Tourist in Africville; or to decry the experience of a people maimed, as Mahlikah Awe:ri in *Dying Breed* – is to sustain, love, protest, and resist.

Whether motivated by a death, a personal struggle, or a collective wrong, the poems in this collection cover a wide range of topics and tonalities. Yet each is also an action in social or political consciousness. Some are emotionally engaged, as Michelle Mae Sutherland in *No Canadian Experience* or Philip Cairns in *Bombing for Peace;* others wry, as Tom Smarda in *Floor Tiles,* Jorge Etcheverry in *Ready & Reddish,* Patrick Connors in *An Open Letter to the Prime Minister;* while the poems of Jeannine Pitas and Osaze Dolabaille are quietly, richly contemplative.

Gender violence is the theme in Candace Dube's poem, *The Same Night;* newcomer experience and exilic memory in the poems of Rashidah Ismaili and Soheila Pashang; class in Don Weitz's self-described rant, *Nameless-Homeless;* and race in Kenji Tokawa's poem of the same name, extracting a resistant counter-text out of a colonialist official document. In *Ode to Mumia Abu-Jamal,* Alys Skel mimics the racist attitude within the U.S. prison system and beyond, showing us its contemporary institutional face; while Ariel David raps on his experience in the Canadian detention system and shares his own (ambiguous) struggle with the sensibility of the street.

The theme of incarceration takes us also to Cuba, or rather, to the U.S., where four of the Cuban Five [see note below] remain in prison. The Cuba section begins with Tomás Aquilino's wistful meditation on Havana, *The Unwritten Song.* Katharine Beeman offers a view of Havana as generous in its spirit in her poem, *What you don't see from the North,* and rallies us to the cause of the Cuban Five. IFPOR is therefore honoured that the two poets among the Cuban Five, Ramón Labañino and Antonio Guerrero, have each offered poems to the anthology, *Poem to a Brother* and *To Love Life,* respectively, both dedicated to the memory of their fallen comrade, Roberto González.

The anthology concludes with poems from a young Communist elected Toronto public school trustee, Elizabeth Hill; a philosophical poet from Sweden, Bengt Berg, sending us his dispatch, *Power Lines;* an American-Canadian social justice activist, Marilyn Lerch, offering us her spin on the tragic (soap) opera, *As the Earth Burns;* and some light verse from an anthology editor in praise of alcohol and love. Finally, the poems of Veronica Eley show poetry as a creative resource for personal survival and possible transformation.

Resistance dignifies. Whether one struggles privately with bi-polar mood disorder or post-traumatic stress, collectively with the memory or present circumstance of a genocide or dispossession, or merely contemplates with irony and distress the corporatization of the global body politic, it is comforting to know that poetry takes a stand, and that words still matter.

If poetry can heal a soul or re-take a city like Medellin, why may it not then flourish its flowers upon the world?

Roger Langen, Editor
Resistance Poetry 2

Note on the Cuban Five – The Cuban Five – Gerardo Hernández, Ramón Labañino, Antonio Guerrero, Fernando González and René González – were the focus of the first IFPOR in 2009. All were involved in reporting on the Cuban-American terrorist network that over several decades has killed 3,500 Cubans, including in the downing of a Cuban aircraft in 1976 by the CIA. Their trial and punishment for "conspiracy to commit espionage" in Miami, Florida, June 2001, is widely regarded as a miscarriage of justice.

About the Cover – Cover art by Gabriele Brossard, Brossard Gallery, Elora, Ontario; www.gabybrossard.com.
Front: "The Fuzzy Woman"
Back: "Veronica's Poem"

Editor's Note – Poem inscribed in "Veronica's Poem" appears in anthology as *Gerstein Centre*.

Acknowledgements – The Editor would like to thank the other members of the Editorial Committee for their advice and support: Lisa Makarchuk, Steve O'Brien, Jeannine Pitas, Carlos Angulo, Jose Gonzalez, and Charles Roach.

James Sugiyama
is a Toronto-based family doctor. His literary sensibility has been influenced by his life-long service to refugee and immigrant populations. He is interested in the connections between health and what he calls the sociopolitical exclusions of poverty and race.

Tourist in Africville

there's a fog over Halifax Harbour
I'm running somewhere
away from the downtown hotel –
at the Navy Yards
I'm apprehended by a guard
'where are you going?'
'Africville'
'huh? ... oh ... it's
up under the Narrows Bridge,'
he nods

there's a fog over Halifax Harbour
the mist obscures Citadel Hill
I slog northward
through a driving rain
past shipyards
and housing projects –
in the distance
a yellow sign,
Africville –
no directions, proclamations
no epitaphs

the cars stream southbound on Barrington Street
horse-carts carry sailors ranting with clap
I hear a tinkling piano –
past a stone gate
onwards, onwards
through the rains
another sign,
Africville

there's a fog over Halifax Harbour
I hear a tinkling piano
I must be hallucinating
I hear a deep bellowing laugh
down by Tibby's Pond
children hunt clams and periwinkles on the tidal flats

a rutted path, weedy grass
clapboard church
on the grey horizon
another sign,
Dog Walking Zone
dogs dancing and sparring
to wake the dead
a cross-burning in Windsor
a race riot in Dartmouth
running water never delivered

there's a fog over Halifax Harbour
on a park bench a tourist sits
Aunt Jessie's garden blooms in wild profusion
in Campbell Road, George Dixon's ghost –
I turn southward, shadowboxing
the unrelenting rain

Migration
(to the Issei)

salmon return to their native brooks
swollen by last night's rains

sitting by the weir
I can sense their urgency
to ascend
some leap metres from the falls
and fall back
into the tail stream

in the waters upstream
a cormorant surfaces
with a fish in his bill
an egret watches
from the willows

I'm sure there is coherence
in my tangled thoughts
as I observe
the struggle home
against odds, predators –
ancient drive to return

to where? ... a birthing place, a dying place
the promise of future
never witnessed
and almost never attained

Michelle Mae Sutherland
is an educator, poet, songwriter, author, and mother of two sons, Lemar and Moses. She has been writing since 2001 and performing and publishing her work since 2007. Her first book of poetry, *Set Free to Soar*, was published in 2012.

No Canadian Experience

this phrase, No Canadian Experience
like the sound of bad, bad music
as we navigate the new land

interviews after interviews
the same bad news
the sound that echoed
the sound that employers use

listen
and you will understand
experienced Computer/Programmer Analyst

hired as a Customer Service Representative
Wal-Mart, CIBC
Telephone Banking Centre
companies that my status qualified me to enter
selling prepaid legal services, cell phones, pagers ...

No Canadian Experience

truly a diplomatic scheme
device to shatter big dreams

I was let go
like Fanon (1991) "assailed at various points"
dislocated and fragmented
zeal replaced with disillusionment

jobless, moneyless
heading down the street to join the homeless

second interview
position of Computer/Programmer Analyst
old racism myth
do you have any Canadian Experience

my response
as a telemarketer
isn't computer software the same in Canada as in Jamaica ... Sir?

No Canadian Experience

the fact that I was black ... a partiality
the fact that I was black ... inexperienced?

the fact that I was black

I resisted
and in that instance
I dismantled hindrance
space was created
I in my blackness made entrance
Computer/Programmer Analyst

Jorge Etcheverry Arcaya
has published criticism and poetry in Canada and abroad. Born in Chile, his six books of poetry, starting with *The Escape Artist* in 1981, are a meditation on lives lived in the consciousness of personal displacement by political forces. His *Chilean Poets: A New Anthology* appeared in 2011.

Ready & Reddish

I share in the purest essential features
of the redneck lifestyle
I hang around pool halls
Not long ago I had a motorcycle
I still like to go to rock concerts at Barrymore's
or the Gilmour for country music
for a chance to dance with a gorgeous Métis girl
In the welfare line-up
or at the boarding house
I've had a talk with a rundown, skid row prophet
This kind of life should lead to a revolution
'Rednecks of America!
Rednecks of Canada and Quebec!
Go red!'

Analogy

The feathers of birds
the carapaces of insects
absorb and block heat and cold
to protect delicate inner tissues
just as warm dwellings are hidden
in all latitudes of earth

This is a law we can extrapolate
to the history of all empires
flourishing in their Capital Cities
in wanton luxury, surrounded
by living walls of flesh
made up of the best men
chosen from the plains and marshes
to defend those cities

The methods have changed
The core remains
the same

Don Weitz
is a longtime "anti-psychiatrist" and social justice activist living in Toronto. The following is an excerpt from his "rant in progress." The poem is dedicated to Edmond Yu, a homeless psychiatric survivor shot dead by Toronto police on a vacated TTC bus in 1997. He credits Allen Ginsberg's poem, *Howl*, for inspiration.

Nameless-Homeless
(a rant in progress)

I see you I hear you
on george & gerrard
in and out of satan house
barred from the schoolhouse

another homeless shelter
the city wants to shut down
save the schoolhouse, save the schoolhouse

I see you I hear you
panning on queen and spadina

I see you I hear you
freaking out
on queen and dufferin
at CAMH on queen and ossington

I see you I hear you
panning harassed by RioCan security guards
at yonge & eglinton
on church and wellesley
mad with your voices

I see you I hear you
evicted on sherbourne and dundas
harassed by cops on king and university

I see you I hear you
black brothers stopped walking or driving
at jane and finch
I see you panning at bay and king
barred for sleeping outside city hall
I see you I hear you
on parliament and gerrard
I see you I hear you
on bloor and spadina
I see you I hear you
on danforth and broadview
I see you I hear you
on bloor and bathurst
I see you I hear you
at queen's park where
mpps and ministers of lies
are deaf and blind to your misery

I see you I hear you
in Hamilton, home of big steel
I see you I hear you in Ottawa
bastion of bigotry, hypocrisy, official lies

I see you I hear you in Sudbury
where union brothers and sisters reach out to us
I see you I hear you
in Winnipeg where first nations brothers
are arrested and jailed, shot at
for drinking, driving, marching
with dreams and visions of a First Nations general strike

I hear you I see you in
Red Deer, Alberta where big oil
threatens your land, your health and your lives
I see you I hear you
in Churchill
freezing your ass off at 40-below
I see you I hear you
in Vancouver's downtown east side
stoned, mad as hell, getting clean in-site needles to survive

I hear you I see you
in Whitehorse
I see you I hear you
in Nunavut where
polar bears are also homeless

OH KANATA

I see you I hear you nameless-homeless
brothers and sisters
all over this fucking stolen land
where harper, mcguinty, ford
and the rcmp
solve homelessness with their final solutions ...

Kenji Tokawa
is a mixed-race Nikkei writer and arts educator based in Toronto, territory of the Haudenosaunee, Wendat, and Anishinaabe. His poem is extracted from the Canadian government Order-in-Council that dispossessed Japanese-Canadians in World War II. The poem was previously published in *Ditch Poetry*.

Race

Order in Council revoking P.C 5523, dated 29th June, 1942
And P.C. 6885, dated 20th July, 1942 – transfer to the Custodian of the property of persons of **the** Japanese **race** evacuated
from the protected areas of B.C.

P. C. 469
AT THE GOVERNMENT HOUSE AT OTTAWA
TUESDAY, the 19th day of JANUARY, 1943.
PRESENT: HIS EXCELLENCY
    THE GOVERNOR GENERAL IN COUNCIL –

    WHEREAS by Order in Council dated 29th June, 1942, (P.C. 5523) amended by Order in Council dated 4th August, 1942, (P.C. 6885) Regulations were made imposing certain duties and responsibilities on the Director of Soldier Settlement of Canada in relation to agricultural lands owned by persons of the Japanese race ordinarily resident in the protected areas of British Columbia;
    AND WHEREAS the Secretary of State reports that the appraisals of lands contemplated by the said Order in Council as amended have been made and that it is the opinion of the Minister of Mines and Resources to whom the Director of Soldier Settlement of Canada reports under the said Order in Council as amended, that the said Order in Council as amended, should be revoked;

That by Order in Council, dated 20th July, 1942, (P.C. 6247) it was provided that on and after the 1st August, 1942, all unfinished business of the Committee under the Chairmanship of the Honourable Mr. Justice Sidney A. Smith of Vancouver, appointed by Order in Council of 13th January, 1942, (P.C. 288) in respect of vessels or equipment vested in the Custodian under the said Order should be transferred to the Custodian, and the Custodian was vested with all vessels and equipment which had not been disposed of under the supervision of the said Committee;

That since the transfer was effected, question has been raised as to the authority of the Custodian to deal with unfinished business of the said Committee in relation to vessels or equipment disposed of prior to the 1st August, 1942, and it is expedient to remove any doubts in this respect;

That by Orders in Council relating to the property of persons of the Japanese race evacuated from the protected area of British Columbia, the Custodian has been vested with the responsibility of controlling and managing property belonging to persons of the Japanese race who have been evacuated from the protected areas, except deposits of money, shares of stock, debentures, bonds or other securities or other property which the owner on being evacuated from the protected areas was able to take with him; and

That the evacuation of persons of the Japanese race from the protected areas has now been substantially completed and that it is necessary to provide facilities for liquidation of property in appropriate cases.

THEREFORE, His Excellency the Governor General in Council, on the recommendation of the

Secretary of State, and concurred in by the Minister of Mines and Resources, the Minister of Pensions and National Health, the Minister of Labour and the Minister of Fisheries, and under the authority of the War Measures Act, Chapter 206 of the Revised Statutes of Canada, 1927, is pleased to order and doth hereby order as follows:

1. Order in Council, dated 29th July, 1942 (P.C. 5523) and amending Order in Council dated 4th August, 1942, (P.C. 6885) are hereby revoked.

2. Paragraphs numbered 3 and 4 in Order in Council dated 20th July, 1942 (P.C. 6247) are hereby rescinded and the following are substituted therefor:

3. The Custodian may, where he considers it advisable to do so, liquidate, sell or otherwise dispose of any such vessels or equipment on such terms and conditions as he deems advisable; and any agreement entered into or document executed by the Custodian on or after August 1, 1942, and prior to the date of this Order, purporting to be an agreement for, or to be, a transfer, conveyance or other disposition of any such vessel or equipment or of any right, title or interest therein is hereby given full legal validity, force and effect as if the Custodian had full power to enter into such agreement or to execute such document, and as if such vessel or equipment or such right, title or interest therein, as the case may be, had been vested in the Custodian, at the time of the entry into such agreement or the execution of such document.

4. Without restricting the generality of the powers hereinbefore conferred, all unfinished

business of the said Committee is hereby transferred to the Custodian and shall be deemed to have been so transferred as on and from the 1st August, 1942.

Whatever, under Orders in Council under the War Measures Act, Chapter 206 of the Revised Statutes of Canada 1927, the Custodian has been vested with the power and responsibility of controlling and managing any property of person of the Japanese race evacuated from the protected areas, such power and responsibility shall be deemed to include and to have included from the date of **the vesting of such** property in the Custodian, the **power** to liquidate, sell, or otherwise dispose of such property and for the purpose of such liquidation, sale or other disposition the Consolidated Regulations Respecting Trading with the Enemy (1939) shall apply mutatis mutandis as if the property be**long**ed to **an enemy** within the meaning of the said Consolidated Regulations.

Certified to be a true copy.

A.D.P. Heeney
Clerk of the Privy Council.

Osaze Dolabaille
is a poet and drummer born in Trinidad. Years after his emigration to Canada, the 'ancestors awakened him to his identity, history and culture – in a word, to his spirituality – as an Afrikan.' He has appeared at community gatherings, spoken word events, and concerts since 1998.

The Power of One

"Can I make a difference?" I wondered aloud
"Can I make a difference, just one face in the crowd?

There's a war that is raging, we are under attack
And if we make some progress we just get beaten back

The Destroyer cuts down our young men in their prime
Our babies have babies long before their time

Our youth can't relate to the elders, it seems
Either thoughts of despair, or unrealized dreams

Our men can't find work for the mouths they must feed
So they run from their families in their time of need

Our women abandoned, on their men place the blame
Then the next generation repeats it again

If we think we've escaped to suburbia and wealth
Then the fear of returning takes a toll on our health

We have tried integration; we have tried to fit in
We just end up wondering why we never win

We've been trained far too well to devalue our own
And without an identity we call strange places home

Africans from all over can tell that it's bad
And this AIDS that they gave us – the whole world has gone mad!

You are wise, O Creator, all-powerful too
But against all this oppression, *what the fuck can I do?*"

It was then that the Spirit told me she had heard
Every angry complaint, every frustrated word

"Yes, you can make a difference; it's already begun
For you have within you the Power of One

This is Power to stand when you're low to the ground
To create, not destroy; to build up, not tear down

It's the knowledge of self and the love of I AM
To shed light on the lies that you learned from the man

Call it ancestral memory, wisdom from above
But know this: I give it to you, Whom I Love

Now the Power of One is the gift of the wise
And when each One can teach One you all will arise

You will gather your people and set their minds free
To imagine-the-nation I want you to be

Reconstructing community, reclaiming the throne
Reconnecting the circle to call it your own

Only then will the joy of the children release
Only then will the elders assemble in peace

And a world that is dying with awe will be filled
And together you will teach them how to rebuild

For the Power of One is true power indeed
When you know, you will not be afraid to succeed."

Then Divine Spirit paused for a moment or two
But when he broke it down for me I knew what to do

"Yes, you can make a difference, just remember my son:
Be sure to continue ...

The Power of One"

Silent Too Long

The drums have been silent too long
Welcomes of rhythm no more
Lifeless skins
Gathering their collective dust
Echoes unseen, recused from reality
Displaced by the dull-witted
Plodding monotone
A white noise
Devoid of articulation
Poured directly onto cracked heads

A voice has been silent too long
Its songs unborn, unheard, unloved
Sore-throated
Sick and swollen tongue
Longing for waters of wisdom
Instead of an ignorant
Mindless braying
That counter-culture
Of huddled masses
Still facing a western sun

This pen has been silent too long
How heavy it now feels!
Poised *poetica*
Overflow of ordnance unleashed
Following final orders of deployment
Along corridors *in utero*
Ever closer
To new beginnings
While seeking souls
Look behind and ahead, together

Mahlikah Awe:ri
is a drum talk, poetic rapologist, Red Slam Collective emcee, Musician and 4 Directions Urban Arts Facilitator of Afro-Native Heritage/Mohawk (Kahnawak:ke) & Mi'kmaw (Bear River). In 2011 she released the EP *Serpent's Skin*. Her poem, "2 Dream in Colour," was published in *Diaspora Dialogues TOK* (6th edition).

Dying Breed

but a dying breed
an editor at Maclean's Magazine writes
but a dying breed

she is ... ?
she is ... ?

despite being the weaver of dreams

beyond forecasted prophecies of
all seeds of creativity

she is ... ?
but a dying breed
but a dying breed

she is ...
like Indian summer
then quickly gone

she locks herself in attics
the elders plead for her
not to cut her hair
she begs her brother
to cut out her tongue
so she can inhale gasoline fumes
in silence

the elders plead for her to join the sweat
smudge away the violence
she can't
she won't
she won't blanket the truth
truth's blanket
heavy as rocks
contaminated with smallpox

she is but a dying breed
she is but a dying breed
she is ...
no round dance speaks
to the soles of her feet
she has no soul

she eats paper
unsigned treaties for breakfast
drinks a cocktail of gin & water laced with lead before bed
instead of prayers
gives head
to blank stares in
piss-drenched alleyways
nameless motels

this is her Pow Wow
this is her gathering

she is but a dying breed
she is but a dying breed

she is ...

and I
I have passed her by
many a millennia

on busy intersections
and random street corners
our eyes meet

I pull away
towards the East
I'm walking away from my sister
away from my sister

away from
My

Sister

Candace Dube
is a Métis activist and strong believer in grassroots resistance. Raised in a small town in northern Ontario, she currently resides in Hamilton, Ontario, with her partner, Julie, and two children, Tayson and Jaxon.

The same night
(to my sons)

because I am a womyn
I seek out safe spaces and places and people

because I am a womyn
I sometimes get scared at night, the same night
when the moon lights the sky and the stars whisper
we'll watch over you tonight

the same night
when one womyn chooses to walk
and take in the starry sky
rather than look at the back seat of a cab
the same night she was raped

the same night he grabbed her from behind, strangled her and took her
life into his hands
where she was abandoned under a transport
pants under her ankles
limp
lifeless and left unconscious in a pool of her own

                                                blood
                                              and urine
                                         and humiliation

and he
he lights a cigarette and walks away

because I am a womyn
this fucking matters

because I am a mother
my sons will know this truth
because I am a womyn
I sometimes get scared at night
because I am a womyn
I seek safe spaces and places and people

Alys Skel
is an underground activist living in Toronto. The subject of her poem is the former Black Panther and president of the Philadelphia Association of Black Journalists, Mumia Abu-Jamal. In 1982 he was convicted on improbable evidence of murdering a policeman. On death row for 29 years, his sentence was commuted in December 2011 to life imprisonment without possibility of parole.

Ode to Mumia Abu-Jamal

you may be innocent of the crime
but one thing you are not innocent of, Sir
is that you are Black

I wear the uniform
and I'm here to remind you
of your nigger place
your place, to remind you
of your place
to remind you and
all of your nigger brothers and sisters
of your place

of your place in our great America
(god-fearing, decent and ... dammit
still White (you nigger fuck

(what is it people can't seem to understand?!

Mumia Abu-Jamal will never go free
because Mumia Abu-Jamal
is Black, goddammit

you may be innocent of the crime, Sir
but I wear the uniform and
I'm here to remind you
I'm here to remind you

Ariel David

[a pseudonym] was born in Toronto. Attracted by gangsta rap and its associated lifestyle, he dropped out of school early and entered the life. Fellow inmates nicknamed him Shady. He is an ongoing survivor of street-level, drug-and-violence mayhem in Toronto, Moncton and Liverpool, England. He describes himself as an "outgoing, self-admitted work in progress."

Metro West

the tall walls make me uncomfortable as I'm shot from every angle
it's a kodak moment
an interpersonal feel without a signed consent
my privacy is strangled
I'm just another man sitting guilty until proven innocent
the cage is claustrophobic and my mind has no choice but to ride along shotgun
he looks for smuggled tobacco to roll a cigarette and asks me
"Yo, you got one?" A simple reply will do as an elongated conversation
seems to always lead to confrontation between me and this man
or the officer manning his station
as I walk the green mile my oversized blue flaps stick to the floor, what a sorry excuse for a shoe passed down from man to man
god only knows the stories that go with them, the sad stories originating from prison to prison
I live in a prism, confused as I follow the lines, how did I get to this point,
locked away, throw away the keys to my
lips, I don't think I'll talk today as I sit in this hole, this empty abyss
the punishment given because I spoke with my fists
born into the wild I once again need to fend for myself
as I did as a child, I've walked miles but ended up at the wrong place
angry men in blue feel the need to compensate for their stolen lunch money, don't laugh, they have the upper hand
you don't even have soap for a bath, so you ask yourself
am I still man?

has this west end place stolen my lunch money, I'm placed in front
of a mirror, faced off with
my masculinity, and fascinated with the man I'm facing
I try to reach through or at least lose my mind
I want to be changing places

Physical intrusion

my mind is stronger than your muscle
you flex to make your point clear
because your go system is pristine
but the frontal lobe screams stop, in front of the cracked mirror
where you find an empty glass, covered in residue. Things seem illusive
This intrusion knows no barrier, adjacent the muscle
so let's try not to spread a subliminal message
I am a hypocrite, as I know nothing else but
the compelling thought of advancing my position in this broken mirror
life as I see it
you should expect the same from me, as I lack character
but the difference is, I am equipped, with the sword in the stone
because I am strong with characteristics that shine without tone
what need have we to speak, when a gesture
is often remanded for its curtain call, when the water's too dark
and you think until your mind sinks too deep
your muscle makes you weak
mine makes me acknowledge your weaknesses –
words are seen by millions
muscle is for minions

The one who left his mind at the station

20 pack of beer, get em in im a crook
spicy cinnamon with an adrenalin strut
a minion in cuffs, shackled hack, im corrupt
back to bat with a black kinda rap, ok enough
it stink like the stuff that comes up from yer bowels
I spit shit, drop exlax with the vowels
im foul, I speak feces, I need a towel & shout
I rip through with weapons that repent from my mouth
philosophize preaching as knees weaken weekly
dream big, speak Nietzsche
proposing a toast and civil war with myself
ouch!
the mind's amiss on arrival, its ritual
running circles im tribal, habitual
aboriginal, simple minded, cynical
freddy krueger slasher but I keep it at a minimal
im Trivial, im jeopardy, I got questions
but hold on, criminal record, oops! forgot to mention
I used to kick it old school, its david beckham
a little bit of English with a foot in yer rectum

Overdose

Where are you?

Are you where I see you standing, or somewhere else?

Am I here standing next to you, or somewhere else with you?

Am I alone?

Where did you go? I don't see you there.

Why is my prescription empty?

Jeannine Pitas
from Buffalo, New York, is a Ph.D. candidate at the University of Toronto's Centre for Comparative Literature. She is the translator of acclaimed Uruguayan poet, Marosa di Giorgio's, *The History of Violets* (Ugly Duckling Presse: Brooklyn, 2010). Her first poetry chapbook, *Our Lady of the Snow Angels*, is forthcoming from Lyrical Myrical Press.

Czeslaw Milosz

for so many years I have studied your language
in the hope of grasping your sharp-edged words
that pierce my fingers like chandelier's crystals
shining above your staircase to the other world

for so many years my eyes have squinted
dazzled by the brightness as I try to step
into the golden-white room you've created
the snow-globe room, that second space you wept for
the halted pendulum of heaven and hell
that your words set in motion again

for so many years I have struggled
to enter that room, spiral up to the magic
mountain where I know the sky will split in two
and the mind, at last, lift its hands

for years I've stood at the bottom
of your mountain, just as you once stood
outside the walls of the Warsaw ghetto,
the name of each life lost
a melting angel in your glove –

you, who were always your brother's keeper
you, who remembered all the wrongs
done to simple men
you, who dared to believe
that the human mind was made
of woods and fields rather than walls

for so many years I have studied your language
as if, in doing so, I might also cross oceans
as if, in doing so, I might also speak words
that turn walls
to melting
snow

Proof

the news came yesterday
you're not real
you were never real
it has finally been proven:
the universe was never cupped inside your hands
the stars were never released from your grip
and we – we were never made
in your image

they've finally expelled you –
you, whom I still turn to
you, whom I still cry out to
even though they tell me
that all along you were a lie

I have inscribed your name
into my palms
I have drawn your face
on this dirtied canvas of my body
I have heard your words
and repeated them
shouting them into the forest
a cathedral without echoes

I walk the winding, wet path
through all these desolate cities
these polluted fields
these bare, sharp-edged mountains
I call you and call you

No más muertes

Stalactites cling
to the insides of mountains

Saguaros stand
like telephone poles, daring bad
drivers to try and knock them down

This is the sunniest
place on earth, some say

They didn't build a fence along the border
They thought the desert
was enough of a wall

And it is. Sonora, Chihuahua, a room
filled with daggers
held out by dry hands

No más muertes. Protestors in Tucson raise
their signs. No more deaths, they exclaim
But the copper-red desert hills
don't listen
and neither does the *migra*

Patrick Connors
has recently performed at the Toronto Poetry Club, and Burrard Inlet Fish Fest. His work has appeared in the inaugural issue of *Chrysalis Magazine* and as part of the Poesie 78 project. He was shortlisted in the 2012 Fermoy International Poetry Competition out of County Cork, Ireland.

An Open Letter to the Prime Minister

first of all, I want to give you
my sincere congratulations

you see, I have voted PC also
(and not just because
they are my initials

my vanity perhaps, some
misplaced appeal to paternalism

but you, only a brilliant opportunist
could turn a vote of non-confidence
into an overwhelming success!

I am an ordinary average guy
I know Joe Walsh songs, listen to Rush
love hamburgers and French fries –
with my boys few conversations begin without
how about them Leafs! or Jays, or Raptors ...
I have hugged far more trees than women
(prefer the latter)

you say
people don't care about art
giving glory to God in any way possible

as long as we don't take a stand
we the people have a hand
in your conservative rhetoric

since we're stuck with each other
I have confidence, Prime Minister
that you and I
can come to some sort of compromise

I will go on reading poetry
and you can go on telling lies

Tom Smarda
is an activist on affordable housing, anti-war, and other social justice issues. During the 1970s he hitchhiked around North America playing music from the Yukon to Guatemala. Witnessing poverty and injustice inspired him to write poetry and songs. He believes that we can house, clothe and feed one another without destroying the Earth.

Horror Story

I sat by myself
On some grass
Behind the stage
Overlooking the military base.

A group of young people
Sat down beside me,
And I became a member
Of their circle,
Holding a vigil and remembrance service
For those who had been
Murdered and tortured
By those trained at the base.

I just sat and sobbed
Uncontrollably with them;
For the loss of loved ones
We all shared.

Floor Tiles

I wonder how much
The person was paid
Who designed the
Pattern along which
The tiles in the
Food court were laid.

Or was the pattern
Computer-generated?

How long did
The software designer
Have to go to school
In order to create
The program
Which would design
The floor tile pattern
In the food court?

Soheila Pashang
is a Professor and Coordinator with the Social Service Worker – Immigrant & Refugee Program at Seneca College. She is the editor of *Unsettled Settlers: Barriers to Integration* (January 2012), offering "strategies for practical interventions" in the lives of "immigrants, refugees, non-status and racialized persons." Her poetry focuses on these and other sociopolitical issues.

Suitcase

ready to depart
suitcase in hand
time passing
mind holding
foot contemplating
and then – a pause

her heart pounding
for the aroma of fresh bread
and the taste of ripe fig
one last glimpse
at the harvest
and a cow grazing in the distance
the pressing grain of wheat
thirsting for the stream
at twilight

slowly
she disappears in sorrow
longing for Eastern breeze
to caress wavy hair dyed with henna
silence
takes her gendered body
on a White journey
away from the whispering of blossoms
where the stem of an apple tree
from grandfather's garden
at the curve of silver-mountain
carefully roots
on the delicate fertility of the suitcase

yet
she's called
from a faraway land
where the red revolutionaries
resisted oppression on Pahlavi street
and their children
marched against illusionary democracy
and seeded the Green movement
on Khomeini street
under the same canopy of maple trees
overarching molten asphalt

here in diaspora
the wounded souls
are left with the memories of
twenty-five millennia of civilization
the stolen history
the heroic narratives
safely domesticated
in Western museums

and there
red tulips and nascent green are confined
beneath the shadow of the tyrant
the threats of global sanction and war
in dark, in solitude
in silence
the choked city awaits
the enemies
lurking under the guise of past pain
to justify present violence

the vein of pomegranate is boiling
under soft skin

Dream

I had a dream, a poignant dream
the night was enraged with tempestuous rain
and thunderbolts coiling giant waves
the sea was unsettled, and so the man
crossed by armed men
moaning in fear, receding from fate –
the ship was floating on a deep sea, resisting the howling wind
the raging swells from the east –
foreseeing his exodus in this ticking night
I saw him being drowned
the sea devouring its prey, in a maelstrom night
I woke up furious, turning to TV for solace
the news described famine in Africa
and child obesity in America
a bomb blast in Europe
and tension erupting in the Middle East
I heard President Obama
cautioning the poor about economic depression
but above all, the reporter calm, smiling, coiffed
keeping dispassionate at all cost

I remembered the young rejected refugee
who I left behind in the confined room
he was desperate to find his report card and ID
to pursue education, to set down roots
under thunderbolts, on floating ships
he clambered up his courage and gazed into my eyes
and with steady voice
that spoke to a life in captivity stated:
"I am not religious and had slept with a man"
I reflected on the reporter
and reflected on the man
and wondered
why can't I calmly smile when writing this poem?

Rashidah Ismaili
teaches Creative Writing at Wilkes University, Pennsylvania. She hosts Salon d'Afrique in Harlem, a cultural "meeting place" of African artists from all over the world. She has authored several books of poetry and has been widely anthologized. The selection below is an excerpt from a much longer poem. She lives in Harlem with her son, an emerging documentary filmmaker.

Attar and Tamirs

She is a rose
splattered
dropped
petal by petal.

A date palm
struggles
under sun
under siege
gives up
its seeds.

Attar
sweetens
smoked air
silt and grime
clogs a nose
daring to inflate.

A torn
one-armed doll
forgotten
lies nude
amongst debris
home reduced
to rubble,
little hands
clutch mother's finger
walks
silent and scared.

2

Roses splattered
beneath
a date palm
whose seeds
dry up
and sun
puckered balls
bespeak negligence.

She is a daughter
who will never
come to cut onions
nor roll her sleeves
whitened with flour.

She is a former
best student
whose books
are closed.
She is success
mounted
on a bare wall.

Allahu Akbar!
a baby cries.
A mother cries.
A father cries.
A brother dies.

Rabbi Rhaman!
The earth shakes.
Dishes shake.
Beds shake.
Oumi shakes.
A house falls.
Ya Azziz!

3

An old great-grandfather house
encircled by ululation,
white encased women,
come to shrill out Shaiytan
come to comfort a mother's heart.

In feet stamp
in hand clap
in circular dance
in sacred words
in collected grief

The Umma comes,
comes wailing, wailing
Ya Azziz! Ya Azziz! Ya Azziz!

Tomás Aquilino López
from Havana, Cuba, is Art Conservator at Factoria Habana, Center for Contemporary Art. *Fragmented Havana*, a selection of his poetry, was published in Toronto, Canada in 2009 by Crocodile Sugar Press.

The Unwritten Song

Every day there are fewer faces
in this city
which silences our cries
of sorrow

A pathetic attempt to triumph by leaving
their hidden marks remain
in every doorway

An unborn child sings
the unwritten song
of a sleepless lunatic
who did his worst for love
and succeeded

Havana
fragmented into whispered canticles of return
into voices that cannot be heard

We must scream louder
into those tides of darkness
that circumscribe
this eternal repetition

Katharine Beeman
Montreal poet, translator and reviser, has published four collections of poetry and contributed to diverse anthologies. She is an active contributor to readings and festivals. She has also been described as "an avid participant in history, rivers and revolutions." The poem below was written after a Texas court exonerated the Cuban-American terrorist, Luis Posada Carriles.

What you don't see from the North

Havana's sky
slow-dancing
all together
the new moon smiles
clouds   black   and white
stars   twinkling   and still
in a generous round
the Drinking Gourd opens its heart
offers to pour

the North Star flees
flinging hand over cup
keeps
its brew bitter

RAP for the Five

(inspired by Bolivian Hortensia Lina Cazón, daughter of the first guerilla fighter of Che's band to fall, and Charles Roach, stalwart in rhyme and revolution)

Heroes guide
points of stars alive
from continents we stride
five fingers of our hands collide
to set them free
glide, birds of liberty
to loved ones' side

Homeland, humanity
Bolivia indigenous pluri-nationality
Cuban doctors help to see
I feel el Che
dancing in his bones today
¡ahora llegamos! I hear him say
no drop of struggle drains away
comrade's wife and daughter, sharing pride
on my Island
standing for the five

Heroes guide
points of stars alive
from continents we stride
five fingers of our hands collide
to set them free
glide, birds of liberty
to loved ones' side
free the 5! free the 5! free the 5! free the 5!
Free the Cuban Five!

Coming home poem
La Puerta

(A small love poem in two languages
En dos lenguas, para tí, un pequeño poema)

If it were the end of the day
no matter the time
and you stepped through my door
if it were the end of the day
and I stepped through your door
no matter the time
if there were a door
my love   mi amor
a kiss   un beso
a hug   un abrazo
love   amor

Antonio Guerrero Rodriguez
is one of the Cuban Five [see Foreword]. His original sentence of life in prison plus ten years was reduced in 2009 to 21 years plus ten months. He has written several books, including poetry. The late, distinguished Angel Augier, Cuban poet, essayist and journalist, describes Antonio Guerrero as having "an irrevocable vocation for liberty."

To Love Life
(dedicated to our brother Roberto)

To love days
of sun and earth
To love the times
that we remember
To love new
and old houses
To love the light
and the darkness
To love paths
and highways
To love valleys
as we love the mountains
To love waves
over the sand
To love the sea
and the shores
To love the patio
and the terrace roof
To love the night
and the storks
To love the moon
and the stars
To love the rain
and the white fog
To love the snow
and the springtime

To love flowers
and the bees
To love the shine
of bottles
To love noise
in the schools
To love prose
and poems
To love the edge
of surprise
To love the dreams
that keep us awake
To love just things
and certainty
To love the world
that contemplates us
To love the homeland
and the flag
To love people
who love and create
To love peace
and never war
To love life
 – and to fight for it!

James Cockcroft
is the author of *WHY? ¿POR QUÉ? POURQUOI? POETRY & POESÍA* (Hidden Brook Press, 2009). He has published poetry in sundry anthologies. His latest of 48 books is *Mexico's Revolution Then and Now* (NY: Monthly Review Press, 2010; also published in Spanish & French). Readings/lectures: jcockcro@yahoo.com, www.jamescockcroft.com.

"¡Daniel vive, carajo!" ("Daniel lives, damn it!")
(in memoriam, Daniel del Solar, 1940-2012)

You took on the toughest part,
that of dying truly,
said merrily, "Live well, die well."

You died like you lived,
beloved friend,
showering us energy high with love and humour.

In those final days and nights,
as a fire consumes a dry forest,
swiftly, inevitably
you resolved life's needs.

With great sensitivity,
consciousness, reconciliation,
generosity of spirit,
love, above all.

You and Ana united
a singular, awe-inspiring tsunami of love, and, yes, rage,
gentleness, humour, wisdom.

And, when needed,
the strategic pause ...
the bathroom seemed oh so far away.

Dancing the morphine dance, Daniel,
tempered your indignation
at capitalism's spiralling crimes
with that smile, oh that smile,
of a deeper knowledge,
from which I still learn.

Go then, Daniel, you who
popped new pills, in that final year,
just to ease the pain,
but told few, so you could go on,
helping friends, expecting nothing in return ...

Your friends Venezuela, the Cuba Five,
alternative media,
political prisoners,
poets of resistance,
lovers old and new,
Quebec in the South,
CELAC, the indignados,
family, Ana, Nina, me ...
mother earth, humanity.

You had new waters to traverse,
untested, unknown though fully sensed,
you, Daniel, with Ana,
overflowed them, us, with beauty.

Each day in Montreal,
I touched your and Ana's
last tangible gift to us,
Latino Eyes, photographs
in the wooden box on my desk ...

I still do, with neither tears nor dry eyes.
silent now before such beauty.

So I will write,
I will organize,
dance, laugh, garden and swim,
for that is what I do ...
and I know you are with me.

¡Daniel vive, carajo!

Ramón Labañino Salazar

is one of the Cuban Five. His sentence of life plus 18 years was reduced in 2009 to 30 years. He was then transferred from Florida to Georgia. Born to a humble family, he graduated *summa cum laude* as an economist from the University of Havana in 1986. He is one of the two poets (with Antonio Guerrero) among the Cuban Five. He has three daughters.

Poem to a Brother
(in memoriam, Roberto González)

you left us too soon
the sun's rays have not yet shone
on the just side of history
you left us between the wafts
of your beloved's first kiss
and those beloved of our own
who still await us ...

this irrational moment, unjust
did not allow us
a last firm embrace
nor place for your clear-eyed and noble gaze
affection radiating from your smile
the background to a Cuban "son" ...

you are now one more score to settle
in the name of dignity, of justice
your strength the strength of just causes
the banner of our souls
of our tenacity
beginning with the dawn of each day

you, a man of honour
to dispute the malice of the universe
the day will yet deliver to us
the great embrace of paradise
in honour of your memory
and we, we will continue to fight!

Lisa Makarchuk
has worked as a newscaster, translator, and DJ on Cuban radio. She is former president of the Canadian-Cuban Friendship Association and has sat on the Free the Five Cultural Committee. She co-chaired the First International Festival of Poetry of Resistance (Toronto) and was Coordinator of the Third IFPOR in 2011, editing the Volume 1 Anthology, *Poetry of Resistance*.

Lest We Forget
(A Chat with Hillary Clinton about U.S. Policies)

we have always been
on the side of The People, she said

did you mean
Lest we forget?

I think Mossadegh
Aristide, Lumumba
Arbenz, Allende
elected, murdered, exiled
or deposed
coups, attempted coups
Brazil, Honduras, Venezuela
just to name a few

I think Iraq, Abu Ghraib, Guantanamo
Viet Nam and My Lai
massacres at the prison
at Daejeon
hundreds of thousands die
Gaza, Shatila
the Philippines, Pakistan
Indonesia and Afghanistan
millions degraded or gone
, all on the side of The People

Lest we forget

white phosphorous, drones
Agent Orange, napalm
cluster bombs, uranium
think Operation Condor, School of the Americas
torture and maiming
too many dictators for naming

think Mubarak, Obama's peacemaker
Blair's force for good
Suleiman
provided with teargas, baton
firearms, tank and cannon
in defence of ... The People

genocide of First Nations
blood of slaves
millions
could have loved but
now they lie

in unmarked graves
no records, no memory
ghosts
on the windowpanes
their struggles with us still

Lest we forget

Bengt Berg

is the author of over 30 books, the first a poetry collection in 1974, *Where the Dream Ends*. He is an award-winning poet and publisher, operating the publishing house, Heidruns Forlag, and Heidruns Book & Art Café in Trosby, Sweden. He frequently collaborates with musicians. His poems, noted for their wry observation, are translated into many languages.

Power Lines

Power lines run
from the sunlight to the earth
to those who once walked here passing by

Power lines run
from the rivers up north
through the dark forests
down to the new districts in the south,
to great structures in a different language

Power lines run
between people,
glowing copper wires that sing in the night,
dark and mute when everything has been said,
green and sprouting like thin roots

Power lines run
between those who rule
and those who try to grab hold of their lives,
power lines between the way it once was
and the way it will one day become

Marilyn Lerch
from East Chicago, Indiana, is a longtime social justice activist living in Sackville, New Brunswick. Her published poetry collections include *Lambs & Llamas, Ewes & Me* (2001), *Moon Loves Its Light* (2004), and *Witness and Resist* (2008). She has taught creative writing in several NB correctional institutions, and was president of the Writers' Federation of New Brunswick, 2006-2010.

As The Earth Burns

A body with an arm whose fingers
hold the handle of a briefcase
keeps close to another body
with an arm whose finger
is allowed to press the button
inside the briefcase

ipso facto
the reach of human power
MAD

in facto
buttons control fingers
because we are only smart enough
to destroy ourselves +

PROGRESS = MORE FINGERS ON MORE BUTTONS

Paul Klee drew "The Twittering Machine"
long before we
became one

Look out!
(your window)
for Humming Birds
hovering
in deepest winter

That Drone you hear
might be your own
Fish(ing) and Chips everywhere

DIGITAL TECHNO-EVOLUTION = TOTAL SURVEILLANCE

One nation
over God
makes it legal
to disappear
its own citizens

Do not send diapers
to a Hamas infant
You may be detained
indefinitely
and tried by a
Military Tribunal

Do not press a coin
into a foreigner's hand,
he may pass it on to someone
labeled "an associated group"

HABEAS CORPUS = DEAD LANGUAGE

Industrial capitalism
broke
the will of men and women
who never saw the sun
and the bodies
of children mangled
in moving parts

Finance capitalism
transforms the commodity money
into monopoly play money
by pressing buttons on a keyboard
which is virtual power

ABSOLUTE VIRTUALITY CORRUPTS ABSOLUTELY

To sum(mon) up:

EMPIRES IN DECLINE = FASCISM IN ASCENDANCE

You heard it first on a Roman Holiday
And that ain't the half of it

Philip Cairns
is an actor/writer/visual artist from Toronto. His work appears in a wide variety of periodicals. He has performed monologues at the Theatre Centre, Gladstone Hotel, and Buddies in Bad Times. His plays have been read at Paddy's Playhouse and Major Space. He is one of the organizers of "The Beautiful and the Damned", a monthly poetry and music series at Zelda's.

Bombing For Peace

The Earth weeps
As the bombs rain down.
Red flashes,
Exploding buildings.
Annihilate the fuckers
In the name of peace.
Outside my building,
Children shriek in the playground.
Whilst in Iraq,
Children scream
In quaking houses
Without basements.
Anti-war protestors
Are slaughtered in the streets.
Today, I don't wish
To be a citizen of this planet.
I'm ashamed to be a part
Of this atrocity.

Haven't the children of the world
Suffered enough?
Presidents issue orders
From ivory towers.
It's unlikely they will be killed
By computerized Cruise Missiles.

Tears wash over Mother Earth.
A feeling of numbness
Flows from my head
To my feet.
Watching bombs exploding
On my TV set
Between moronic commercials
And soap operas
Cast with pretty faces
Of both genders.
Flashes of pink lightning
In the sky.
Mushroom clouds of destruction.
I'm ashamed to be a citizen
Of this planet.

Severed limbs flying
Through the sky.
A baby's bloody head zooms
Into the air
And lands at his mother's feet.
Little girls run
Screaming down country roads
As napalm explodes
In the background.
Race versus race,
Killing in the name of peace.
Bayonets plunge into firm bellies.
Green guts ooze from
The crimson wounds.
"Let's kill another Gook
For Jesus."

Rainbow bombs detonate
In a far off city.
My mind freezes in apoplexy.
Shall we kill another child
For peace?
I don't want to live
On a planet like this.

Cold tears cascade
Over the Earth,
Cleansing it of its bitter past.
I wish I lived in a world
Where peace has ruled for countless centuries.
Is that too much to ask?

Elizabeth Hill
grew up in the west end of Toronto during the Cold War. Her father was a union carpenter and her mother a housewife and activist for peace and women's rights. She joined the Young Communist League while still in high school. In 1988, she was elected a public school trustee, serving in this role for 18 years. She is President of the Canadian-Cuban Friendship Association, Toronto.

Assumptions Are Made

It is assumed we are all men
That we all speak English
And drive cars
And eat meat
And can walk up stairs
And we go to church on Sundays
And sleep with the opposite sex
And have "flesh coloured" skin

But the reality of our world is not the assumption
And we are all better for it

Veronica Eley
born Manchester, England, was raised in Antigonish, Nova Scotia, and settled in Toronto. She has worked as a secretary at York University, housing worker at Nellie's Hostel and Woodgreen Community Centre, and literacy instructor with the Toronto District School Board. Her poetry arises from her life-long personal struggle with mental illness.

Grey blanket

earliest memory
driving along
a country road
in the back seat
wrapped
in a grey blanket
in the dark

separation
the sidebars
on the hospital bed
two years' old
pneumonia

fifteen-year old girl
raped
police declare
emotionally disturbed
wrapped
in a grey blanket
taken home

disturbed
turbulent
the waters
the waves, the waves
are big, mommy
the cold, grey ocean
is deep
I lean against the railing
of the White-Star Cunard liner
seven years' old

railings
grey blanket
grey, grey

Feelings

swept under a rug
worn as undergarments
I keep
a part of myself
hidden

in the quicksand
of my soul
these feelings
lie like objects
a knife
a hatchet

I am a volcano
red hot liquid
burns my inner psyche
swirling, whirling

making me
unpredictable
a threat
a potential monster

inside out
outside in
the feelings have become
statues in the garden
monuments to a crime

Gerstein Centre

spiritual oasis, isolation ward
a warm and friendly house
clean and orderly
I saw
anorexia
a statement of revolt
schizophrenia
a tight-mouthed stare
ritualistic protective behaviour
necklaced to the point of strangulation
depression
lying around stretched out
suicidal attempts
the day after
no bars or barriers
a lot of lonely people
holding a small candle
on their journeys
I reach out to one
little black girl
anorexic
symbol of our future
God help us
thank you
I am still human

Roger Langen
is Irish-French-Maliseet from Perth-Andover, New Brunswick. Educated in Toronto and Newfoundland, he works as an Executive Officer with the Ontario Secondary School Teachers' Federation, Toronto. Author of *Your Guide to Better Chess* (Coles Notes), he switched to poetry and human rights in 2000. He now looks forward to the endgame in Palestine of a single secular state.

Life's mysteries

how is it the tiger lily
has got a crush on the old bear
where will he wear her, we think
if not around his ear
what will she say to him there
what will he think
to reply

perhaps love belies them both
their ages and their kind

A short history of the world in drink

beer tills the settled land
turned anciently away from the forest
putting grain in the glass
on the rough-hewn table

to the Socratic dialogues of the city
wine gives the sparkle of truth

coffee is for thought,
tea empire

coke softens the whole
with the faint, bubbling clicks
of corporate interiors

while somewhere along the line
Captain Beefheart, Jim Beam and
other rogues in full career
still offer their own brand or cure
for personal insanity

For peat's sake

if I want sugar
I'll take it from a bog
which has hidden bodies
to make its liquor
and offers it to me dry
wiith an honest bite on the tongue

French-Maliseet-Irish et cetera
(Wolastoq, 1813)

in the battle of blue and brown eyes
of light with dark skin
through forest and furrow and all things between
we are in the end
kin

PIFPOR

About IFPOR

The International Festival of the Poetry of Resistance, Toronto, was established by a group of writers, artists, academics and others committed to social justice activism. The aims of the organization are: to plan and promote an annual international poetry festival on social justice themes; to liaise with and support other such festivals and movements around the world; and to assist in the development and publication of a resistance poetry anthology.

IFPOR 2009 was dedicated to Freedom for the Cuban Five; successive events called for freedom for Mumia Abu-Jamal and Leonard Peltier, and for "oppressed people everywhere." IFPOR 2012, Against State Terror, offers solidarity to those abused by the power of the State, whether a whole population as in Gaza, a gathering of G20 protesters in Canada, or a political prisoner like Liliany Obando in Colombia, a labour activist in the world's most dangerous place for trade union activism.

IFPOR asserts the values of international law and human rights. It therefore resists the culture of war: the use of force or the threat of force, under ethical subterfuge like the "responsibility to protect," to advance the agenda of the global corporate elite: by blockades, "covert operations," extra-judicial assassinations, sanctioning of torture, bombing of civilians: — the rough instruments for the procurement of resources; productive only of misery and injustice, and ultimately racist. IFPOR believes a better world is possible.

* * *

IFPOR acknowledges the formative influence of Lisa Makarchuk and Maria Elena Mesa, later Carlos Angulo and Charles Roach (and others). IFPOR acknowledges also the on-going generous support of philanthropist and social activist, Juan Carranza.

The logo on the spine and back cover shows a fisted P, design by Frank Saptel. For more information about IFPOR, go to www.poetryofresistance.org.